Healthy, Quick & Easy JUICING

Healthy, Quick & Easy JUICING

Dana Angelo White, MS, RD, ATC

Publisher Mike Sanders
Editor Brook Farling
Book Designer Jessica Lee
Book Packager XAB Design
Art Director and Photographer Nigel Wright
Food Stylist Ellie Jarvis
Development Editor Rick Kughen
Proofreader Lorraine Jerram
Indexer MFE Editorial Services

First American Edition, 2020
Published in the United States by DK Publishing
6081 E. 82nd Street, Indianapolis, IN 46250

ISBN 978-1-4654-9336-1

A catalog record for this book
is available from the Library of Congress.

Library of Congress Catalog Number: 2020931151

DK books are available at special discounts when purchased
in bulk for sales promotions, premiums, fund-raising, or
educational use. For details, contact:
SpecialSales@dk.com

Printed and bound in China

Photograph on page 5 © Dana Angelo White
All other images © Dorling Kindersley Limited

For the curious

www.dk.com

ABOUT THE AUTHOR

Dana Angelo White MS, RD, ATC is a registered dietitian, nutrition consultant, and nutrition expert for FoodNetwork.com where she is the founding contributor for the website's Healthy Eats blog. As an author, Dana has written seven cookbooks including *Healthy Air Fryer Cookbook*, *Healthy Instant Pot Cookbook*, *Healthy Vegan Air Fryer Cookbook*, and *Healthy, Quick & Easy Smoothies*. Dana is also a sports dietitian and associate clinical faculty in the Department of Athletic Training and Sports Medicine at Quinnipiac University in Hamden, Connecticut. She owns and operates Dana White Nutrition (danawhitenutrition.com) where she offers nutrition counseling, recipe development and analysis, and food education for athletes.

ACKNOWLEDGMENTS

It is so exciting to add another title to the "Healthy, Quick & Easy" series. As an author, I feel truly spoiled by the talented team at DK Books. I am so grateful for the all-star team of editors lead by Brook Farling and Nigel Wright, as well as the talented designers, stylists, and recipe testers.

All of my recipe testing happens from my home office so I need to thank my family for their everlasting patience. They are no strangers to extra grocery deliveries, loud noises, and plenty of dirty dishes! All three of my kids, especially my oldest, Madeline, were always willing to be adventurous, engaged, and critically honest recipe testers. A special shout-out to the local farmers in Connecticut, especially the Gazy family—so many of my recipes are inspired by your weekly harvests.

CONTENTS

INTRODUCTION

Juices are trending again! This nutritious and healthy way of eating lives up to the hype in so many ways. Juicing plant-based foods is a fantastic way to energize, hydrate, and get more fruits and vegetables into your daily routine.

As a dietitian, I have dabbled with juicing for years but only recently started making more juices for my family of five. We juice in my house about three times a week, sometimes for breakfast and sometimes as an after-school snack. Our juicing frequency gets bumped up in the summer when our local farm share and backyard garden have lots of fresh ingredients for us.

We started with basic juice blends like Pineapple Blackberry (pp. 28–29) and Blueberry Granny Smith (p. 43), then expanded to fruit and veggie combo blends like Cucumber Watermelon Sipper (p. 96) and Electric Mango (p. 101), which is made with mango, celery, watercress, and lime. I also get excited about adding unexpected ingredients like teas, spices, and seltzer water, which are combined with other juiced ingredients to create fun and fresh takes on traditional juices (Strawberry Celery Hibiscus Chiller [pp. 98-99] is a perfect example).

Juicing recipes often can be really bulky, cumbersome, and expensive. I have seen recipes with upwards of 10 ingredients, and I'm not a fan, so my primary goal for the recipes in this book was to keep things simple and affordable. None of the recipes feature more than five ingredients, but all are hydrating and flavor-forward. From classic juices, to shots, to juice-tea infusions, I have worked hard in this book to push the limits of what healthy juicing can be, while always keeping in mind seasonality, affordability, nutrient content, and, of course, taste! I hope you are excited, inspired, and most of all, nourished by these recipes.

Dana White

Dana Angelo White

PART 1

· · · · · · · · · · · · ·

JUICING

BASICS

WHY JUICING?

Juicing is a quick, easy, and flavorful way to diversify your intake of plant-based foods including fruits, vegetables, herbs, and spices.

Juicing helps unlock one of the most overlooked qualities of fruits and vegetables—hydration! Juicing also helps unlock many cell-protecting antioxidants that give fruits and vegetables their unmistakable colors and flavors.

I don't treat juices as replacements for eating fruits and vegetables, I treat them as another way to enjoy them and also stay hydrated. While juicing provides ample doses of vitamins and minerals, some nutrients can be lost or destroyed via the juicing process. But don't look at this as a bad thing. By adding juicing to your daily nutrition, you'll be improving your hydration and also getting even more nutrients than if you were consuming only whole ingredients.

A NOTE ON RECIPE YIELDS

The recipe yields in this book are approximate and can vary based on several factors. The type and quality of produce you use can have a significant impact on how much juice a recipe yields; produce that is small or less ripe can have a lower water content and can reduce the amount of juice produced. Ingredients like chili peppers, passion fruit, or bananas can impart a lot of flavor to recipes, but they won't yield much juice. The yield of a recipe can also be impacted by the extraction power of the juicing machine you're using.

JUICING FAQS

What can I juice?
Most fruits, vegetables, and herbs can be run through the juicer, but always check the manufacturer's recommendations for your machine. I encourage you to experiment!

Should I peel my produce?
While you can and should leave the peels on some fruits and vegetables, others must be removed so as not to damage your juicer. Fruits like pineapple, citrus, melon, mango, and banana should always be peeled, while fruits like cucumber, apples, pears, peaches, plums, and even kiwi fruit can be juiced with the skins on. Sweet potatoes are a gray area, but I typically peel them. Check the instructions within each recipe to see if specific ingredients should be peeled.

What should I do with all of that pulp?
Don't toss that delicious pulp; it's all edible! Consuming the pulp from juicing can help you take full advantage of all the nutrient content in your produce, plus it helps reduce food waste in your kitchen. There are several ways to reuse juicer pulp; you can incorporate carrot and cucumber pulp into veggie burgers, apple or celery pulp can be added to baked goods like muffins, or you can steep any combo of fruit or vegetable pulp in water and strain it for a sippable hot tea or nourishing broth. If repurposing pulp in recipes is not appealing to you, the pulp can always be composted.

Can I meal prep juices for the week?
Homemade juices are highly perishable and are best consumed right away. Some juices will begin to oxidize and turn brown in a matter of minutes, but don't worry—the juice is still completely safe to drink. If juices are stored in an airtight container and filled all the way to the top, they can last in the fridge for up to two days; just be sure to give them a good shake before drinking. Some of the blended recipes made with teas and water can be made in larger batches and stored in the fridge for longer. You can also freeze prepared juices in ice cube trays to add them to smoothies. (We love to make juice pops by freezing leftover juices in popsicle molds.)

JUICING 101

At its foundation, juicing isn't complicated—chop the ingredients, toss them in the juicer, and sip away. But there are a few things that are good to know as you begin to add juicing to your daily routine.

CHOOSING PRODUCE

I am often asked if all produce used for juicing should be organic, and you may be surprised by my answer. Organic produce is available year-round and at a higher price point when out of season, but you should choose to buy organic only for produce with edible skins, such as apples, peaches, berries, tomatoes, and some varieties of cucumber. You can save money by buying these items when they are in season. For produce like citrus, melon, and pineapple, there is no need to buy organic because you aren't juicing and consuming the skins.

More importantly, in my opinion local produce ALWAYS trumps organic produce. Because most local farms use safer and more sustainable farming practices, and often grow more unique varieties than large industrial farms, you are not being exposed to the same sorts of virulent chemicals that the industrial farms use. Some smaller farms simply can't afford to be certified organic (even though they follow similar standards), so don't rule out sourcing produce from local farms, even if they aren't certified organic.

CHOOSING A JUICER

Juicers come in all shapes, sizes, and price points. When shopping for a juicer, look for a machine that doesn't have a ton of tiny parts that need to be cleaned, as these can be very difficult and time-consuming to clean. Look for a machine with ample capacity for holding pulp, as this will prevent the need to frequently empty the machine while juicing. Wide feeding chutes are also helpful because they allow you to reduce the amount of time spent chopping ingredients. Check online reviews carefully and look for models that are quieter; some machines are VERY noisy and that's no fun for your household on busy weekday mornings.

(The recipes in this book were created using the Breville BJE200XL Compact Juice Fountain 700-Watt Juice Extractor, and I love it. It is reasonably priced, powerful, and easy to clean.)

TIPS FOR KEEPING YOUR JUICER CLEAN

Here are a few simple tips that will keep your machine clean and your juices tasting fresh.

- Keep the juicer clean! The large parts of most machines are easy to clean, and most machines disassemble easily; most parts are dishwasher safe.
- Scrub the inner disc filter basket after every use. Use a brush to remove any food particles from the fine mesh walls.
- When finished juicing (or even in between juices), run a small amount of water through the machine with the machine running. This will help flush out any remnants of colors or flavors in the machinery.
- Juice smaller or harder-to-juice ingredients first, then run ingredients with a higher water content through last to help ensure you flush out all the flavor as well as any residue.

THE TOP INGREDIENTS FOR JUICING

From nutrition power to delicious drinkability, here are some of the very best ingredients for juicing.

INGREDIENT	BENEFITS
Apples	Crisp, sweet, and tangy all at the same time, fresh apple juice puts the bottled versions to shame.
Beets	Featuring outstanding color and an unmistakable earthy flavor, this root veggie is also filled with natural nitrates to help lower blood pressure.
Carrots	The sweetest and possibly most coveted veggie for juicing, carrots also offer plenty of the antioxidant beta-carotene.
Celery	Celery imparts fresh flavor and color! The feathery leaves also contain blood pressure–lowering compounds.
Cucumber	A super-hydrating veggie that adds the perfect hint of floral sweetness. Keep the skins on for some potassium, magnesium, and vitamin K.
Ginger	Ginger is your juicing secret weapon! This spicy element can elevate any juice, plus it has the benefit of promoting healthy digestion.

INGREDIENT	BENEFITS
Mango	I am obsessed with this delightful tropical fruit. Mango makes the most delicately sweet nectar that is perfect to blend with any veggie.
Parsley	Parsley adds tons of herbaceous goodness for a small number of calories. It's also packed with vitamins and minerals including vitamins A, C, and K, as well as folate and iron.
Pears	Pears make juices extra frothy, and add vitamins K and C, along with copper and potassium.
Sweet Potato	Even sweeter than you would imagine, this veggie makes the best high-nutrient shooters.
Watermelon	Sweet as candy and ultra-refreshing. The white part of the rind contains special blood-fortifying compounds, so be sure to add some to the juicer.

HELPFUL NUTRITION BOOSTS

You can target specific nutrients to meet your nutrition needs by adding these healthy boosts to your juices. Note that these are added after juicing and should not be added to the juicer.

INGREDIENT	BENEFITS
Chia, flaxseed	Inflammation-fighting omega-3s
Brewed coffee, tea	Caffeine
Chia, coconut milk	Thicker juice
Spirulina, tea, cocoa, cinnamon, cardamom	Extra antioxidants
Spirulina	Extra minerals
Flax, chia, chicory root	Fiber

A NOTE ON FIBER CONTENT

Each recipe in this book features a nutrition breakdown, but note that the fiber content is omitted from the breakdowns. Since the pulp that remains in the machine contains the majority of the fiber, the remaining fiber accounts for such a very small amount per serving that it cannot be accurately quantified, so it's been omitted.

PART 2

· · · · · · · · · · · · · ·

FRUIT
JUICES

PINK GRAPEFRUIT APPLE

As apple season winds down, citrus season picks up, and this juice is my ode to the short time when the two seasons overlap. The addition of the apple helps mellow out the acidity of the grapefruit.

Makes: about 2 servings
Serving size:
7fl oz (205ml)

1 large pink or ruby
 red grapefruit,
 peeled
1 medium Gala
 apple, stemmed,
 cored, and halved

1 Add the grapefruit to the juicer, followed by the apple.

2 Pour into two glasses and serve.

 84 CALS PER SERVING   **5 MIN**    **2 INGREDIENTS**

Nutrition per serving
0g fat (0g saturated fat), 0mg cholesterol, 1mg sodium,
22g carbohydrate, 1g protein

GREEN APPLE CRISP

Keep the doctor away with a tall glass of green apple.
This super-simple juice is crisp and refreshing, and the
apples offer quercetin, a plant compound with powerful
anti-inflammatory properties.

Makes: about 2 servings

Serving size:
 8fl oz (235ml)

4 medium Granny
 Smith apples,
 stemmed, cored,
 and halved

1 Add the apples to the juicer.

2 Pour into two glasses and serve.

 **160 CALS**
PER SERVING

 3 MIN

 **1 INGREDIENT**

Nutrition per serving
0g fat (0g saturated fat), 0mg cholesterol, 0mg sodium,
44g carbohydrate, 0g protein

WILD WATERMELON

This single-ingredient juice is wildly refreshing. Peel away the watermelon's green skin, but include the white rind because it's filled with an antioxidant called citrulline, which helps improve circulation.

Makes: about 2 servings

Serving size:
12fl oz (355ml)

4 cups cubed watermelon, white rind included

1 Add the watermelon to the juicer.

2 Pour into two glasses and serve.

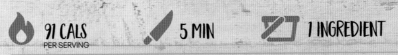

91 CALS
PER SERVING

5 MIN

1 INGREDIENT

Nutrition per serving
0g fat (0g saturated fat), 0mg cholesterol, 4mg sodium, 23g carbohydrate, 2g protein

KIWI CANTALOUPE

Did you know kiwi fruit peels are edible? They're included in this recipe to help add a few extra minerals as well as a bit of tartness to the sweet cantaloupe.

Makes: about 2 servings

Serving size:
 8fl oz (235ml)

4 cups chopped
 cantaloupe

2 medium kiwi fruit,
 unpeeled

1 Add the cantaloupe to the juicer, followed by the kiwi fruit.

2 Pour into two glasses and serve.

 **155 CALS** PER SERVING   **5 MIN**    **2 INGREDIENTS**

Nutrition per serving
1g fat (0g saturated fat), 0mg cholesterol, 53mg sodium,
38g carbohydrate, 4g protein

GRAPE GETAWAY

Juiced grapes are incredibly sweet, so that beautiful sweetness is cut a bit with creamy coconut milk and then poured over ice to create a cool, refreshing drink that has a tropical feel.

Makes: about 2 servings

Serving size:
 10fl oz (295ml)

1 cup seedless green
 grapes

2 cups
 unsweetened,
 unflavored coconut
 milk

2 lime wedges

1 Add the grapes to the juicer.

2 Pour into two glasses with ice and add a cup of coconut milk to each glass. Squeeze a lime wedge into each glass, stir, and serve.

 76 CALS PER SERVING

5 MIN

 **3 INGREDIENTS**

Nutrition per serving
4g fat (4g saturated fat), 0mg cholesterol, 50mg sodium,
9g carbohydrate, 0g protein

MANGO BERRY PUNCH

This deep purple juice is designed to promote heart health. It's rich in antioxidants and potassium, and it contains 15 percent of your daily iron needs.

· ·

Makes: about 2 servings

Serving size:
  8fl oz (235ml)

2 cups diced extra-
  ripe mango

2 cups fresh
  blueberries

1 large green apple,
  stemmed, cored,
  and halved

1 Add the mango to the juicer, followed by the blueberries and apple.

2 Pour into two glasses and serve.

 **240 CALS** PER SERVING   **5 MIN**    **3 INGREDIENTS**

Nutrition per serving
1g fat (0g saturated fat), 0mg cholesterol, 4mg sodium,
61g carbohydrate, 3g protein

PINEAPPLE BLACKBERRY

This blend is a dynamic duo for cardiovascular health. Blackberries contain more heart-protecting antioxidants than most other berries, and pineapple contains bromelain, an inflammation-fighting enzyme.

Makes: about 2 servings

Serving size:
 6fl oz (175ml)

6oz (about ½ pint)
 fresh blackberries

2 cups chopped
 fresh pineapple

1 Add the blackberries to the juicer, followed by the pineapple.

2 Mix gently with a spoon, pour into two glasses, and serve.

 119 CALS PER SERVING

 **5 MIN**

 **2 INGREDIENTS**

Nutrition per serving
0g fat (0g saturated fat), 0mg cholesterol, 3mg sodium,
30g carbohydrate, 2g protein

PEACH NECTARINE OJ

This sweet and tangy fruit nectar tastes like a summer dessert! Leave the skins of the peaches intact; they'll add flavor, nutrients, and a dynamite color. This blend supplies almost 10 percent of your daily iron needs.

Makes: about 2 servings

Serving size:
8fl oz (235ml)

4 medium unpeeled
  peaches, pitted

2 medium unpeeled
  nectarines, pitted

2 medium oranges,
  peeled

1 Add the peaches to the juicer, followed by the nectarines and oranges.

2 Pour into two glasses and serve.

 **242 CALS** PER SERVING

 5 MIN

 **3 INGREDIENTS**

Nutrition per serving
1g fat (0g saturated fat), 0mg cholesterol, 0mg sodium,
58g carbohydrate, 6g protein

GRAPEFRUIT TANGERINE PEAR

Meet your new breakfast addiction! This blend of bright citrus and mellow pear makes a delightfully frothy drink, and it delivers all your daily vitamin C needs.

Makes: about 2 servings

Serving size:
 8fl oz (235ml)

1 large pink
 grapefruit, peeled
 and halved

2 large tangerines,
 peeled

1 medium pear,
 stemmed, cored,
 and halved

1 Add the grapefruit to the juicer, followed by the tangerines and pear.

2 Pour into two glasses and serve.

 150 CALS PER SERVING

 5 MIN

 **3 INGREDIENTS**

Nutrition per serving
1g fat (0g saturated fat), 0mg cholesterol, 3mg sodium,
39g carbohydrate, 2g protein

CRANBERRY PINEAPPLE COCKTAIL

Cranberry is extremely sour all by its lonesome, but when it's teamed with juicy pineapple, the result is a frothy and complex cocktail that is incredibly refreshing.

Makes: about 2 servings

Serving size:
 6fl oz (175ml)

1 cup (about 3oz)
 raw cranberries

3 cups chopped
 fresh pineapple

1 Add the cranberries to the juicer, followed by the pineapple.

2 Mix gently with a spoon, pour into two glasses, and serve.

152 CALS PER SERVING   5 MIN   2 INGREDIENTS

Nutrition per serving
0g fat (0g saturated fat), 0mg cholesterol, 2mg sodium,
37g carbohydrate, 1g protein

GUAVA KIWI BERRY

What's not to love about a pretty pink juice that is blushing with sweet flavor and color? Don't let the guava's tough seeds scare you off; they can be processed in the juicer.

Makes: about 2 servings

Serving size:
 6fl oz (175ml)

2 small guavas,
 peeled and
 quartered

3 large kiwi fruit,
 peeled

2 cups fresh
 strawberries, hulled
 and sliced

1 Add the guavas to the juicer, followed by the kiwi fruit and strawberries.

2 Pour into two glasses and serve.

 **177 CALS** PER SERVING

 10 MIN

 **3 INGREDIENTS**

Nutrition per serving
2g fat (0g saturated fat), 0mg cholesterol, 7mg sodium,
41g carbohydrate, 5g protein

STRAW NANA ORANGE

This juice is tangy, refreshing, and the most delightful shade of fuchsia. This blend contains hefty doses of vitamin C, a powerful antioxidant.

Makes: about 2 servings

Serving size:
 8fl oz (235ml)

1lb (450g) fresh
 strawberries, hulled

1 medium banana,
 peeled

1 medium navel
 orange, peeled

1 Juice the strawberries, followed by the banana and orange.

2 Mix gently, pour into glasses, and serve.

 168 CALS PER SERVING

 3 MIN

3 INGREDIENTS

Nutrition per serving
1g fat (0g saturated fat), 0mg cholesterol, 3mg sodium,
42g carbohydrate, 3g protein

ABC (APPLE BANANA CLEMENTINE)

This fruity trio is smooth, drinkable, and can be made year-round. This juice is best consumed immediately because the banana will start to turn brown relatively quickly.

Makes: about 2 servings

Serving size:
 6fl oz (175ml)

2 medium apples (any variety), stemmed, cored, and halved

1 medium banana, peeled

2 clementines, peeled

1 Add the apples to the juicer, followed by the banana and clementines.

2 Pour into two glasses and serve.

186 CALS PER SERVING

5 MIN

 **3 INGREDIENTS**

Nutrition per serving
0.5g fat (0g saturated fat), 0mg cholesterol, 3mg sodium, 48g carbohydrate, 1.5g protein

LEMONY TANGERINE MELON

This juice takes on a smoothie-like texture, and the flavor bursts in your mouth with every vitamin C-filled sip. Also, cantaloupe is a good source of beta-carotene, which makes this juice ideal for your complexion.

Makes: about 2 servings

Serving size:
 8fl oz (235ml)

1 medium lemon,
 peeled

2 tangerines, peeled

3 cups diced
 cantaloupe

1 Add the lemon to the juicer, followed by the tangerines and cantaloupe.

2 Pour into two glasses and serve.

 130 CALS PER SERVING

 10 MIN

 **3 INGREDIENTS**

Nutrition per serving
1g fat (0g saturated fat), 0mg cholesterol, 37mg sodium,
34g carbohydrate, 3g protein

STRAWBERRY APPLE FIZZ

Fresh strawberry juice has the most amazing flavor, and it's only enhanced by adding apple. A little fizz from a flavored seltzer helps turn this blend into the perfect mocktail!

Makes: about 2 servings

Serving size:
10fl oz (295ml)

3 cups fresh
  strawberries, hulled

1 large Gala apple,
  stemmed, cored,
  and halved

1 cup flavored,
  unsweetened
  seltzer (lime,
  pineapple, or any
  of your choice)

1 Add the strawberries to the juicer, followed by the apple.

2 Pour into two glasses, gently stir half of the seltzer into each glass, and serve.

 127 CALS PER SERVING

 5 MIN

 3 INGREDIENTS

Nutrition per serving
1g fat (0g saturated fat), 0mg cholesterol, 3mg sodium,
32g carbohydrate, 2g protein

PAPAYA MANGO COOLER

This tropical juice combo is ideal for breakfast or brunch, plus the papaya contains a special enzyme that promotes healthy digestion.

Makes: about 2 servings

Serving size:
8fl oz (235ml)

2 cups chopped
extra-ripe papaya
(about 1 medium)

2 cups chopped
ripe mango
(about 1 medium)

1 Add the papaya to the juicer, followed by the mango.

2 Pour into two glasses and serve.

 **161 CALS** PER SERVING

 5 MIN

 2 INGREDIENTS

Nutrition per serving
1g fat (0g saturated fat), 0mg cholesterol, 14mg sodium,
40g carbohydrate, 2g protein

CHERRY LIME APPLE

Cherries are famous for their antioxidant powers. Anthocyanins (the compounds that give cherries their special color) have been linked to decreased risks of cardiovascular disease and cancer. Fresh cherries are only in season for a short time, so don't miss the chance to make this truly special juice.

Makes: about 2 servings

Serving size:
 8fl oz (235ml)

1 cup fresh cherries, pitted

1 medium lime, peeled

3 medium unpeeled Gala apples, stemmed, cored, and halved

1 Add the cherries to the juicer, followed by the lime and apples.

2 Pour into two glasses and serve.

 **229 CALS**
PER SERVING

 10 MIN

 **3 INGREDIENTS**

Nutrition per serving
1g fat (0g saturated fat), 0mg cholesterol, 4mg sodium, 60g carbohydrate, 2g protein

BLUEBERRY GRANNY SMITH

This beverage is blueberry heaven in a glass! The banana adds very little volume, but it brings some texture and a hint of banana essence. For an even sweeter juice, use Gala or Pink Lady apples.

• •

Makes: about 2 servings

Serving size:
6 fl oz (175ml)

2 cups fresh
  blueberries

2 medium unpeeled
  Granny Smith
  apples, stemmed,
  cored, and halved

1 medium banana,
  peeled

1 Add the blueberries to the juicer, followed by the apples and banana.

2 Pour into two glasses and serve.

160 CALS PER SERVING   **5 MIN**   **3 INGREDIENTS**

Nutrition per serving
0.5g fat (0g saturated fat), 0mg cholesterol, 1mg sodium,
41g carbohydrate, 2g protein

BLOOD ORANGE HONEYDEW

Two of my all-time favorite fruits are combined to create this frothy, dreamy juice blend, which has the perfect balance of sweet and tart. I highly recommend doubling the recipe and making ice pops to extend the blood oranges' short season!

Makes: about 2 servings

Serving size:
 6 fl oz (175ml)

3 cups chopped
 honeydew melon

1 large blood orange,
 peeled

1 Add the melon to the juicer, followed by the blood orange.

2 Pour into two glasses and serve.

 104 CALS
PER SERVING

 5 MIN

2 INGREDIENTS

Nutrition per serving
0g fat (0g saturated fat), 0mg cholesterol, 31mg sodium,
26g carbohydrate, 2g protein

APRICOT MELON COOLER

One serving of this frothy juice helps muscles recover after a workout. For an extra burst of refreshment, add half an unpeeled cucumber (hothouse or English-style) to this blend.

Makes: about 2 servings

Serving size:
 12fl oz (355ml)

3 medium apricots, pitted

4 cups chopped cantaloupe

1 medium orange (any variety), peeled

12fl oz (355ml) plain seltzer

1 Add the apricots to the juicer, followed by the cantaloupe and orange.

2 Pour into two glasses, top each with half of the seltzer, and serve.

 177 CALS PER SERVING

 5 MIN

 **4 INGREDIENTS**

Nutrition per serving
1g fat (0g saturated fat), 0mg cholesterol, 52mg sodium,
43g carbohydrate, 4g protein

GINGER PLUM GRAPE

This special drink features a subtle floral edge from the fresh plums, and it's the most magnificent shade of magenta. Ginger beer is non-alcoholic, aids in digestion, and also adds a bit of sweet fizz.

••

Makes: about 2 servings

Serving size:
 8fl oz (235ml)

3 medium plums,
 pitted

1 cup seedless green
 grapes

1 cup ginger beer

1 Add the plums to the juicer, followed by the grapes.

2 Add half of the ginger beer to each of two glasses, pour the juice into the glasses, and serve.

130 CALS
PER SERVING

5 MIN

3 INGREDIENTS

Nutrition per serving
1g fat (0g saturated fat), 0mg cholesterol, 0mg sodium,
29g carbohydrate, 2g protein

INVIGORATING PASSION FRUIT ORANGE

This flavorful combination is perfect when poured over ice and slowly sipped. Don't let the slimy passion fruit seeds scare you away! The juicy seeds are the edible parts and they impart enormous flavor to this drink.

Makes: about 2 servings

Serving size:
5fl oz (150ml)

2 medium navel
  oranges, peeled

1 medium passion
  fruit, halved and the
  seeds scooped out
  (discard everything
  but the seeds)

1 Add the oranges to the juicer, followed by the passion fruit seeds.

2 Pour into two glasses and serve.

 95 CALS PER SERVING

 5 MIN

 **2 INGREDIENTS**

Nutrition per serving
0g fat (0g saturated fat), 0mg cholesterol, 3mg sodium,
24g carbohydrate, 2g protein

RED RASPBERRY RED APPLE

These fruits are extremely different, yet the flavors complement each other beautifully. My kids absolutely love this blend, especially when I add a hint of fresh ginger!

Makes: about 2 servings

Serving size:
 6fl oz (175ml)

6oz (170g) fresh red
 raspberries
 (about 1½ cups)

3 medium apples,
 any variety,
 stemmed, cored,
 and halved

½-inch piece fresh
 ginger root

1 Add the raspberries to the juicer, followed by the apples and ginger root.

2 Pour into two glasses and serve.

 **186 CALS** PER SERVING

 5 MIN

 **3 INGREDIENTS**

Nutrition per serving
1g fat (0g saturated fat), 0mg cholesterol, 4mg sodium,
48g carbohydrate, 2g protein

DOUBLE PEAR

Juicy pears make the most delectably frothy juice. To ensure the pears are ripe enough, check the necks by pressing next to the stems; they should give to gentle pressure. This juice browns quickly, so enjoy it promptly.

Makes: about 2 servings

Serving size:
 6fl oz (175ml)

2 large very ripe
 pears, (about
 1lb/450g),
 stemmed, cored,
 and halved
 (Bartlett variety
 recommended)

1   Add the pears to the juicer.

2   Pour into two glasses and serve.

96 CALS PER SERVING   **3 MIN**   **1 INGREDIENT**

Nutrition per serving
0g fat (0g saturated fat), 0mg cholesterol, 2mg sodium,
25g carbohydrate, 1g protein

PINEAPPLE GUAVA BLISS

Sweet pineapple is the perfect counterpart to fresh guava, which has more than 600 percent of your daily vitamin C needs. Vitamin C is a potent antioxidant that also helps maintain the collagen in your skin.

Makes: about 2 servings

Serving size:
6fl oz (175ml)

2 cups chopped
 fresh pineapple

2 small guavas,
 peeled and
 chopped

1 Add the pineapple to the juicer, followed by the guava.

2 Pour into two glasses and serve.

 131 CALS PER SERVING   **5 MIN** 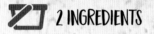 **2 INGREDIENTS**

Nutrition per serving
1g fat (0g saturated fat), 0mg cholesterol, 7mg sodium,
31g carbohydrate, 3g protein

PART 3

· · · · · · · ·

VEGETABLE JUICES

CARROT RED BELL PEPPER

With more vitamin C than oranges, bell peppers are illness-squashing, inflammation-fighting superfoods. Ginger adds an element of perkiness and helps make this juice even more potent for fighting off illness.

Makes: about 2 servings

Serving size:
 8fl oz (235ml)

2 medium red bell
 peppers, stemmed
 and seeded

1lb (450g) carrots,
 peeled and
 trimmed

2-inch piece fresh
 ginger root, peeled

1 Add the bell peppers to the juicer, followed by the carrots and ginger root.

2 Pour into two glasses and serve.

 112 CALS PER SERVING

5 MIN

 **3 INGREDIENTS**

Nutrition per serving
0g fat (0g saturated fat), 0mg cholesterol, 127mg sodium, 27g carbohydrate, 3g protein

TOMATO JUICE WITH BASIL AND SEA SALT

The refreshing blend of tomato and basil is the quintessential summertime combo! Cucumber imparts volume and flavor without adding a lot of calories.

● ●

Makes: about 2 servings

Serving size:
 12fl oz (355ml)

1 cup fresh basil
 leaves

1 medium unpeeled
 English cucumber

1lb (450g) fresh
 beefsteak
 tomatoes, halved

Sea salt, to taste

1 Add the basil to the juicer, followed by the cucumber and tomatoes.

2 Pour into two glasses, sprinkle each serving with sea salt to taste, and serve.

79 CALS PER SERVING   **5 MIN**   **4 INGREDIENTS**

Nutrition per serving
0.5g fat (0g saturated fat), 0mg cholesterol, 135mg sodium,
18g carbohydrate, 4g protein

ULTIMATE TOMATO JUICE

Tomatoes are rich in the antioxidant lycopene, and processing them in the juicer actually helps enhance their cell-protecting power. This two-ingredient recipe is best suited for large and plump garden-fresh tomatoes.

Makes: about 2 servings

Serving size:
 12fl oz (355ml)

1½lb (680g) fresh
 tomatoes, halved
 (heirloom variety
 suggested)

Sea salt, to taste

1 Add the tomatoes to the juicer.

2 Pour into two glasses, sprinkle each serving with sea salt to taste, and serve.

 61 CALS PER SERVING

5 MIN

 2 INGREDIENTS

Nutrition per serving
0.5g fat (0g saturated fat), 0mg cholesterol, 75mg sodium,
13g carbohydrates, 3g protein.

LEMON BEET AGAVE ELIXIR

There is no denying the health benefits of beets, but the earthy flavor can be a turn-off to some. However, when combined with the spark of lemon and a touch of sweetness from the agave nectar, this vitamin-rich scarlet juice is absolutely delicious.

Makes: about 2 servings

Serving size:
 6fl oz (175ml)

4 medium beets
 (about 12oz/340g),
 peeled

1 medium lemon,
 peeled

2 tsp agave nectar

1 Add the beets to the juicer, followed by the lemon.

2 Add the agave nectar and stir well. Pour into two glasses and serve.

 119 CALS PER SERVING

 5 MIN

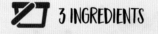 **3 INGREDIENTS**

Nutrition per serving
0.5g fat (0g saturated fat), 0mg cholesterol, 155mg sodium,
29g carbohydrate, 4g protein

CARROT TOMATO LEMON SHOOTER

Need a little pick-me-up? This tangy concoction is meant to be sipped and will give you an instant shot of energy.

Makes: about 2 servings

Serving size:
3fl oz (90ml)

3 large carrots,
  peeled (about
  ¼ lb [115g])

1 medium beefsteak
  tomato

½ medium lemon,
  peeled

1 Add the carrots to the juicer, followed by the tomato and lemon.

2 Pour into two glasses and serve.

 **60 CALS** PER SERVING   **5 MIN**    **3 INGREDIENTS**

Nutrition per serving
0g fat (0g saturated fat), 0mg cholesterol, 78mg sodium,
14g carbohydrate, 2g protein

CRAZY PURPLE CARROT

Carrots come in all shapes, sizes, and colors, but the purple varieties—commonly found in farmers' markets—feature a mild sweetness and also contain antioxidants that come from that natural purple hue.

Makes: about 2 servings
Serving size:
 8fl oz (235ml)

4 medium purple
 carrots, trimmed
 and unpeeled

1 medium unpeeled
 English cucumber

1 medium Granny
 Smith apple

1   Add the carrots to the juicer, followed by the cucumber and apple.

2   Pour into two glasses and serve.

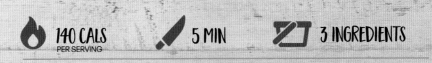

140 CALS PER SERVING   **5 MIN**   **3 INGREDIENTS**

Nutrition per serving
0g fat (0g saturated fat), 0mg cholesterol, 103mg sodium,
35g carbohydrate, 3g protein

CARROT MINT LEMON REFRESHER SHOT

Sweet and tangy with a cool, minty finish—this shot of orange will spark your energy levels and deliver a boost of vitamin C and beta-carotene.

Makes: about 2 servings

Serving size:
 2.5fl oz (75ml)

½ medium lemon, peeled

5 fresh mint leaves

2 large carrots

1 Add the lemon to the juicer, followed by the mint leaves and carrots.

2 Pour into two shot glasses and serve.

 39 CALS PER SERVING

 5 MIN

 3 INGREDIENTS

Nutrition per serving
0g fat (0g saturated fat), 0mg cholesterol, 53mg sodium, 9g carbohydrate, 1g protein

SIMPLY CARROT

This simple juice is bursting with beta-carotene and is how I introduce people to homemade veggie juices because it is undeniably delicious. Those feathery green carrot tops are also edible and overflowing with nutrients, so add a few to the juicer if you have them.

Makes: about 2 servings

Serving size:
  8fl oz (235ml)

8 large carrots,
  scrubbed and
  trimmed (about
  2lb/900g)

1 cup roughly
  chopped carrot
  tops (optional)

1 Add the carrots to the juicer, followed by the carrot tops (if using).

2 Pour into two glasses and serve.

 89 CALS PER SERVING

 **2 MIN**

 **1 INGREDIENT**

Nutrition per serving
0g fat (0g saturated fat), 0mg cholesterol, 149mg sodium,
21g carbohydrate, 2g protein

SWEET GOLDEN BEET

Bright yellow golden beets are ideal for juicing because they're sweet and less earthy than traditional red beets. You'll be dazzled by the vibrant color and sweet flavor of this juice.

Makes: about 2 servings

Serving size:
8fl oz (235ml)

1½lb (680g) golden beets, peeled and halved

2 large carrots, peeled

2-inch piece fresh ginger root, peeled

½ medium lemon, peeled

1 Add the beets to the juicer, followed by the carrots, ginger root, and lemon.

2 Pour into two glasses and serve.

99 CALS
PER SERVING

10 MIN

4 INGREDIENTS

Nutrition per serving
0g fat (0g saturated fat), 0mg cholesterol, 115mg sodium, 24g carbohydrate, 3g protein

CUCUMBER MINT COOLER

Make a large batch of this super-refreshing and low-calorie juice! There are plenty of nutrients in the cucumber skin, but it can impart a bitter taste. If you use the wrapped hothouse variety, you don't have to peel the cukes.

Makes: about 2 servings

Serving size:
12fl oz (355ml)

2 medium unpeeled hothouse or English cucumbers

½ cup fresh mint leaves (about 10 leaves)

1 Add the cucumbers to the juicer, followed by the mint leaves.

2 Mix gently with a spoon, pour into two glasses, and serve.

45 CALS PER SERVING   **3 MIN**   **2 INGREDIENTS**

Nutrition per serving
0g fat (0g saturated fat), 0mg cholesterol, 6mg sodium, 11g carbohydrate, 2g protein

TOMATO MINT CELERY

This Bloody Mary–inspired blend features a hint of optional prepared horseradish for a snappy kick. If possible, include the leaves on the celery stalks because they're super flavorful.

Makes: about 2 servings

Serving size:
 8fl oz (235ml)

1lb (450g)
 tomatoes, halved

2 celery stalks

5 fresh mint leaves

1 tsp prepared
 horseradish
 (optional)

1 Add the tomatoes to the juicer, followed by the celery and mint leaves.

2 Pour into two glasses, stir half of the prepared horseradish into each glass, and serve.

 46 CALS PER SERVING

 5 MIN

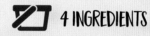 **4 INGREDIENTS**

Nutrition per serving
0.5g fat (0g saturated fat), 0mg cholesterol, 26mg sodium,
10g carbohydrate, 2g protein

CUCUMBER LEMON

This bright, yet mellow, low-carb juice helps fight thirst and aids in hydration, and the celery salt helps boost the flavor without adding too much extra sodium.

Makes: about 2 servings

Serving size:
 10fl oz (295ml)

1 medium lemon,
 peeled

2 medium unpeeled
 English cucumbers

2 tsp honey

⅛ tsp celery salt

1 Add the lemon to the juicer, followed by the cucumbers.

2 Pour into two glasses, stir a teaspoon of the honey into each glass, and serve sprinkled with a light dusting of the celery salt.

 45 CALS PER SERVING   **5 MIN**    **4 INGREDIENTS**

Nutrition per serving
0g fat (0g saturated fat), 0mg cholesterol, 40mg sodium,
12g carbohydrate, 1g protein

SPICY GARDEN SPLASH

This healthier take on a Bloody Mary delivers a hint of heat and a burst of fresh tomato flavor. To dial down the heat, you can remove the inner ribs and seeds from the chili pepper (be sure to wear gloves when handling the pepper).

Makes: about 2 servings

Serving size:
   8fl oz (235ml)

2 medium beefsteak tomatoes (or any other in-season variety)

1 medium cucumber

1 small chili pepper (serrano or red jalapeño recommended), stemmed

1 Add the tomatoes to the juicer, followed by the cucumber and chili pepper.

2 Pour into two glasses and serve.

 46 CALS PER SERVING

 5 MIN

 **3 INGREDIENTS**

Nutrition per serving
0g fat (0g saturated fat), 0mg cholesterol, 9mg sodium, 10g carbohydrate, 2g protein

SPICY CARROT CUCUMBER

If you like spicy, this juice is for you! The capsaicin in chili peppers is known to help increase metabolism. To dial down the heat, remove the ribs and seeds from the jalapeño before juicing (be sure to wear gloves when handling the pepper).

Makes: about 2 servings

Serving size:
 10fl oz (295ml)

½ medium jalapeño
 pepper

1 medium unpeeled
 English cucumber

1lb (450g) carrots,
 peeled

1 Add the jalapeño to the juicer, followed by the cucumber and carrots.

2 Pour into two glasses and serve.

 117 CALS
PER SERVING

 5 MIN

 3 INGREDIENTS

Nutrition per serving
0g fat (0g saturated fat), 0mg cholesterol, 159mg sodium,
28g carbohydrate, 3g protein

BEET CUCUMBER ELIXIR

This low-calorie combination is hydrating, nourishing, and helps fight high blood pressure with the naturally existing nitrates in both the beets and the parsley. For a more citrusy note, use orange blossom honey.

Makes: about 2 servings

Serving size:
8fl oz (235ml)

2 medium beets, peeled

1 medium unpeeled English cucumber

1 cup fresh parsley

2 tsp honey

1 Add the beets to the juicer, followed by the cucumber and parsley.

2 Pour into two glasses. Stir a teaspoon of the honey into each glass and serve.

 **90 CALS** PER SERVING   **5 MIN**    **4 INGREDIENTS**

Nutrition per serving
0.5g fat (0g saturated fat), 0mg cholesterol, 84mg sodium, 21g carbohydrate, 3g protein

SWEET POTATO ZUCCHINI

Zucchini is an incredibly versatile vegetable that adds a slightly sweet but delicate flavor to this juice. One serving of this blend contains 15 percent of your daily recommended iron.

Makes: about 2 servings

Serving size:
 5fl oz (150ml)

2 medium zucchinis

1 medium sweet
 potato, peeled and
 chopped

1 Add the zucchinis to the juicer, followed by the sweet potato.

2 Pour into two glasses and serve.

 83 CALS PER SERVING

🔪 **3 MIN**

 **2 INGREDIENTS**

Nutrition per serving
0.5g fat (0g saturated fat), 0mg cholesterol, 40mg sodium,
18g carbohydrate, 3.5g protein

ZUCCHINI TOMATO WITH BOK CHOY

This low-calorie drink delivers a dose of hydration, vitamin C, and potassium. The delicate color will fade pretty quickly, so this juice is best served right out of the juicer.

Makes: about 2 servings

Serving size:
  8fl oz (235ml)

1 large beefsteak
  tomato, halved

1 medium unpeeled
  zucchini, chopped

2 cups chopped bok
  choy

1 cup fresh parsley

1 Add the tomato to the juicer, followed by the zucchini, bok choy, and parsley.

2 Pour into two glasses and serve.

 70 CALS PER SERVING   **10 MIN**    **4 INGREDIENTS**

Nutrition per serving
1g fat (0g saturated fat), 0mg cholesterol, 68mg sodium,
13g carbohydrate, 4g protein

TOMATO PARSNIP AND PARSLEY

Parsnips look like white carrots, but they pack a spicier bite and mingle beautifully with milder carrot and tomato. Parsley adds a bright, green flavor to make this drink perfectly balanced.

• •

Makes: about 2 servings

Serving size:
6fl oz (175ml)

1 large beefsteak
tomato, halved

2 large parsnips,
peeled

2 large carrots,
peeled

2 cups fresh parsley

1 Add the tomato to the juicer, followed by the parsnips, carrots, and parsley.

2 Pour into two glasses and serve.

117 CALS PER SERVING

5 MIN

4 INGREDIENTS

Nutrition per serving
1g fat (0g saturated fat), 0mg cholesterol, 90mg sodium,
26g carbohydrate, 4g protein

CELERY BELL PEPPER PICK-ME-UP

This elixir gives celery juice a sweet edge with some vitamin C-rich bell pepper. As a general rule, a pound of celery will yield about 1½ cups of juice.

Makes: about 2 servings

Serving size:
8fl oz (235ml)

1 medium red bell pepper, stemmed and seeded

1lb (450g) celery hearts

1 Add the bell pepper to the juicer, followed by the celery hearts.

2 Pour into two glasses and serve.

 **55 CALS** PER SERVING

5 MIN

 **2 INGREDIENTS**

Nutrition per serving
0.5g fat (0g saturated fat), 0mg cholesterol, 183mg sodium, 11g carbohydrate, 2g protein

FIZZY CUCUMBER PUNCH

This hydrating, low-calorie punch is refreshing and delicious. Make a big batch to serve at holiday parties or as a hydrating beverage for hot summer days!

Makes: about 6 servings

Serving size:
 8fl oz (235ml)

2 medium unpeeled
 English cucumbers

1-liter (34fl oz) bottle
 orange or berry-
 flavored, unsweetened
 seltzer water

½ cup optional fresh
 herbs (mint, basil, or
 parsley suggested)

1 Add the cucumbers to the juicer.

2 Combine the cucumber juice and seltzer in a large pitcher, then gently stir.

3 Pour the mixture into glasses filled with ice. Add the fresh, whole herbs, (if using), and serve.

 15 CALS PER SERVING

5 MIN

 **3 INGREDIENTS**

Nutrition per serving
0g fat (0g saturated fat), 0mg cholesterol, 2mg sodium,
4g carbohydrate, 0g protein

BEET RED BLEND

This concoction of fiery red veggies is blended into a slightly sweet and acidic juice with an earthy finish. This combo promotes healthy skin and helps optimize circulation.

● ●

Makes: about 2 servings

Serving size:
 8fl oz (235ml)

1 large beefsteak
 tomato, halved

2 large beets,
 peeled

2 medium red bell
 peppers, stemmed
 and seeded

1-inch piece fresh
 ginger root, peeled

1 Add the tomato to the juicer, followed by the beets, bell peppers, and ginger.

2 Pour into two glasses and serve.

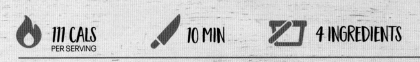

111 CALS PER SERVING   **10 MIN**   **4 INGREDIENTS**

Nutrition per serving
0.5g fat (0g saturated fat), 0mg cholesterol, 60mg sodium,
25g carbohydrate, 4g protein

GREEN PEPPER CUCUMBER

A little green pepper adds vitamin C and a pleasantly sharp
kick to mildly sweet cucumber juice.

Makes: about 2 servings

Serving size:
  8fl oz (235ml)

1 medium unpeeled
  English cucumber

1 medium green bell
  pepper, stemmed,
  halved, and seeded

1 Add the cucumber to the juicer, followed by
      the green bell pepper.

2 Pour into two glasses and serve.

42 CALS PER SERVING   **3 MIN**   **2 INGREDIENTS**

Nutrition per serving
0g fat (0g saturated fat), 0mg cholesterol, 5mg sodium,
10g carbohydrate, 2g protein

HOT CARROT CELERY

If you like heat, this juice is for you! It's bursting with carrot flavor and the heat of jalapeño, which adds capsaicin—the compound that gives peppers their fiery edge. For a less-spicy version, remove the seeds and membranes from the jalapeño.

Makes: about 2 servings

Serving size:
 8fl oz (235ml)

1lb (450g) carrots, trimmed

1lb (450g) celery hearts

1 jalapeño pepper, stemmed

1 Add the carrots to the juicer, followed by the celery hearts and jalapeño.

2 Pour into two glasses and serve.

 112 CALS
PER SERVING

 5 MIN

 **3 INGREDIENTS**

Nutrition per serving
0g fat (0g saturated fat), 0mg cholesterol, 103mg sodium,
25g carbohydrate, 3g protein

CARROT CELERY TOMATO

This recipe is reminiscent of V8 juice, but it is so much fresher and sodium-free. If you like a hint of spiciness, hit this with a few dashes of hot sauce or Worcestershire sauce.

Makes: about 2 servings

Serving size:
 8fl oz (235ml)

1lb (450g) carrots,
 peeled

1lb (450g) celery
 hearts

1 large tomato
 (beefsteak or
 heirloom varieties),
 quartered

1 Add the carrots to the juicer, followed by the celery hearts and tomato.

2 Pour into two glasses and serve.

125 CALS PER SERVING

5 MIN

3 INGREDIENTS

Nutrition per serving
0.5g fat (0g saturated fat), 0mg cholesterol, 165mg sodium,
27g carbohydrate, 4g protein

LEMON-LIME CARROT AGAVE FUSION

This is like carrot juice and lemonade had a beautiful, sippable baby! One serving of this juice provides about 20 percent of your daily potassium needs.

Makes: about 2 servings

Serving size:
 8fl oz (235ml)

1 medium lemon, peeled

1 medium lime, peeled

8 medium carrots, scrubbed and trimmed

2 tsp agave nectar

1 Add the lemon to the juicer, followed by the lime and carrots.

2 Pour into two glasses, stir a teaspoon of the agave nectar into each glass, and serve.

 133 CALS PER SERVING

5 MIN

4 INGREDIENTS

Nutrition per serving
0g fat (0g saturated fat), 0mg cholesterol, 69mg sodium, 34g carbohydrate, 3g protein

PART 4
· · · · · · · · · · · ·
COMBO
JUICES

PINEAPPLE SPIRULINA

Spirulina is a form of dried tropical algae that is ground into a fine powder. It's bursting with nutrients like iron, magnesium, and vitamins A and K, and it is the most spectacular color.

Makes: about 2 servings

Serving size:
8fl oz (235ml)

4 cups chopped
  fresh pineapple

1 tsp blue spirulina
  powder

1 Add the pineapple to the juicer.

2 Stir in the spirulina powder and mix well.
Pour into two glasses and serve.

 **167 CALS** PER SERVING

 5 MIN

 **2 INGREDIENTS**

Nutrition per serving
0.5g fat (0g saturated fat), 0mg cholesterol, 16mg sodium,
44g carbohydrate, 3g protein

RAZ LEMONADE

Store-bought pink lemonade typically contains sugar and artificial colors. This version gets its natural sweetness and delicate pink color from fresh raspberries. You can also substitute strawberries or blackberries.

Makes: about 2 servings

Serving size:
 12fl oz (355ml)

1 medium lemon, peeled

6oz (170g) fresh raspberries

20fl oz (590ml) cold water

2 tbsp honey

2 lemon slices, to serve

1 Add the lemon to the juicer, followed by the raspberries.

2 Add the water and honey, then stir until the honey is dissolved.

3 Pour into two glasses with ice and serve garnished with the lemon slices.

 116 CALS PER SERVING

 5 MIN

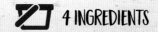 **4 INGREDIENTS**

Nutrition per serving
0.5g fat (0g saturated fat), 0mg cholesterol, 2mg sodium, 30g carbohydrate, 1g protein

CUCUMBER APPLE

Rich in magnesium and vitamin K, this simple juice blend is a powerhouse for promoting healthy muscles and blood. This is an awesome choice for a daily, low-calorie pick-me-up.

Makes: about 2 servings

Serving size:
8fl oz (235ml)

2 medium apples (Gala or McIntosh), stemmed, cored, and halved

1 medium unpeeled English cucumber

1 Add the apples to the juicer, followed by the cucumber.

2 Pour into two glasses and serve.

139 CALS PER SERVING

5 MIN

2 INGREDIENTS

Nutrition per serving
0g fat (0g saturated fat), 0mg cholesterol, 5mg sodium, 36g carbohydrate, 1g protein

CUCUMBER WATERMELON SIPPER

Warning! This big glass of crispy cucumber and subtly sweet watermelon is addictive and contains only 100 calories! Be sure to include some of the white watermelon rind, which contains the coveted amino acid citrulline.

Makes: about 2 servings
Serving size:
 12fl oz (355ml)

1 medium unpeeled
 English cucumber

4 cups cubed
 watermelon

1 medium lime,
 peeled

1 Add the cucumber to the juicer, followed by the watermelon and lime.

2 Pour into two glasses with ice and serve.

 101 CALS PER SERVING   **10 MIN**    **3 INGREDIENTS**

Nutrition per serving
0.5g fat (0g saturated fat), 0mg cholesterol, 7mg sodium,
26g carbohydrate, 3g protein

BROCCOLI APPLE SURPRISE

Broccoli juice might seem like a choice only for die-hard juicing enthusiasts, but you will be pleasantly surprised by the sweet tastiness of this broccoli and apple blend.

Makes: about 2 servings

Serving size:
 8fl oz (235ml)

12oz (340g) broccoli
 florets and stems
 (about 1 bunch)

2 apples, stemmed,
 cored, and halved
 (Gala variety
 recommended)

1 cup fresh parsley

Juice of ½ lemon

1 Add the broccoli to the juicer, followed by the apples and parsley.

2 Pour into two glasses, stir equal amounts of the lemon juice into each glass, and serve.

162 CALS PER SERVING   **10 MIN**   **4 INGREDIENTS**

Nutrition per serving
1g fat (0g saturated fat), 0mg cholesterol, 49mg sodium,
40g carbohydrate, 4g protein

STRAWBERRY CELERY HIBISCUS CHILLER

This pink potion is spiked with a brewed herbal tea. This drink screams of summer but should be enjoyed year-round!

Makes: about 2 servings

Serving size:
 6fl oz (175ml)

1 cup fresh
 strawberries, hulled

½lb (225g) celery
 stalks

1 cup brewed
 hibiscus tea, cooled

1 Add the strawberries to the juicer, followed by the celery stalks.

2 Whisk in the tea, pour into two glasses, and serve.

 41 CALS
PER SERVING

 10 MIN

3 INGREDIENTS

Nutrition per serving
0g fat (0g saturated fat), 0mg cholesterol, 91mg sodium,
9g carbohydrate, 1g protein

BEET APPLE CARROT

This trio of fruits and veggies strikes the ideal balance of sweet, tart, and earthy flavors. Even more impressive are the ample amounts of skin-protecting beta-carotene.

● ●

Makes: about 2 servings

Serving size:
  6fl oz (175ml)

1 medium beet, peeled

1lb (450g) medium carrots, trimmed

2 medium red apples, stemmed, cored, and halved (Gala variety recommended)

1 Add the beet to the juicer, followed by the carrots and apples.

2 Pour into two glasses and serve.

206 CALS PER SERVING

5 MIN

3 INGREDIENTS

Nutrition per serving
1g fat (0g saturated fat), 0mg cholesterol, 190mg sodium, 49g carbohydrate, 3g protein

ELECTRIC MANGO

This combination is sweet, tangy, and the best shade of neon green! Mango contains vitamins A, C, and B6, while watercress delivers vitamin K for blood and bone health.

Makes: about 2 servings

Serving size:
8fl oz (235ml)

2 cups diced fresh mango

1lb (450g) celery hearts

4oz (110g) watercress

2 lime wedges

1 Add the mango to the juicer, followed by the celery hearts and watercress.

2 Pour into two glasses and serve with a squeeze of fresh lime.

 147 CALS PER SERVING

 5 MIN

 **4 INGREDIENTS**

Nutrition per serving
1g fat (0g saturated fat), 0mg cholesterol, 103mg sodium, 32g carbohydrate, 5g protein

PEACH TURMERIC GINGER TEA

This flavorful tea and juice blend is delicious unsweetened but can be sweetened if desired. A pinch of black pepper helps to activate the antioxidants in the turmeric.

Makes: about 2 servings

Serving size:
10fl oz (295ml)

2 medium peaches, pitted and roughly chopped

2-inch piece fresh turmeric root, peeled (or ⅛ tsp ground turmeric, added after juicing)

1-inch piece fresh ginger root, peeled

2 cups freshly brewed white or green tea

Pinch black pepper

2 tsp honey or agave (optional)

1 Add the peaches to the juicer, followed by the turmeric and ginger.

2 Pour the juice into two glasses, then stir a cup of the tea into each glass, add sweetener (if using), and serve over ice.

36 CALS PER SERVING

10 MIN

5 INGREDIENTS

Nutrition per serving
0g fat (0g saturated fat), 0mg cholesterol, 8mg sodium,
8g carbohydrate, 0g protein

ORANGE POM CHIA

With only naturally sweet ingredients, this satisfying and frothy mixture is an awesome way to fight a sugar craving. Chia seeds help thicken the mixture and add a dose of inflammation-fighting omega-3s.

Makes: about 2 servings

Serving size:
12fl oz (355ml)

1-inch piece fresh ginger root, peeled

2 medium navel oranges, peeled and halved

2 cups pomegranate juice

4 tsp chia seeds

1. Add the ginger root to the juicer, followed by the oranges.

2. Stir in the pomegranate juice and the chia seeds. Pour into two glasses and serve.

 **253 CALS** PER SERVING

 5 MIN   4 INGREDIENTS

Nutrition per serving
4.5g fat (0.5g saturated fat), 0mg cholesterol, 11mg sodium, 52g carbohydrate, 4g protein

VANILLA BLUEBERRY CANTALOUPE

Adding natural extracts to juices helps boost flavor while imparting no additional calories. In this recipe, vanilla rounds out the tangy berries and pairs nicely with the playful flavor of the cantaloupe.

Makes: about 2 servings

Serving size:
  6fl oz (175ml)

2 cups chopped
  cantaloupe

2 cups fresh
  blueberries

¼ tsp vanilla extract

1   Add the cantaloupe to the juicer, followed by the blueberries.

2   Mix in the vanilla extract, pour into two glasses, and serve.

 136 CALS PER SERVING   **5 MIN**    **3 INGREDIENTS**

Nutrition per serving
0.5g fat (0g saturated fat), 0mg cholesterol, 26mg sodium,
34g carbohydrate, 2.5g protein

PINEAPPLE CBD

CBD oil has anti-inflammatory properties and offers several potential health benefits, including pain relief. It also imparts a wonderfully smoky and nutty flavor to juices, especially when paired with pineapple.

Makes: about 2 servings

Serving size:
 8fl oz (235ml)

4 cups diced fresh
 pineapple

¼ tsp CBD oil

2 lime wedges

1 Add the pineapple to the juicer.

2 Pour the juice into two glasses, stir half of the CBD oil into each glass, then add a squeeze of fresh lime juice to each glass. Stir again and serve.

 169 CALS
PER SERVING

 5 MIN

 **3 INGREDIENTS**

Nutrition per serving
1g fat (0g saturated fat), 0mg cholesterol, 4mg sodium,
43g carbohydrate, 2g protein

FIERY CARROT

Jump-start your day with a spicy kick of cayenne! This sippable batch of sweet heat will help clear out your sinuses and give you a hefty dose of beta-carotene.

Makes: about 2 servings

Serving size:
 8fl oz (235ml)

8 large carrots, scrubbed and trimmed (about 2lb/900g)

½ medium lemon, peeled

2 pinches cayenne pepper

2 tsp honey

1 Add the carrots to the juicer, followed by the lemon.

2 Pour into two glasses. Add a pinch of the cayenne and a teaspoon of the honey to each glass, stir, and serve.

 165 CALS PER SERVING

 5 MIN

 **4 INGREDIENTS**

Nutrition per serving
0g fat (0g saturated fat), 0mg cholesterol, 199mg sodium, 41g carbohydrate, 3g protein

COCONUT PINEAPPLE BASIL

This juice can promote soft tissue and bone health. Fortified coconut milk imparts vitamin D and calcium, while pineapple and basil contain several inflammation-fighting and cell-protecting antioxidants.

• •

Makes: about 2 servings

Serving size:
  8fl oz (235ml)

1 cup fresh basil
  leaves

3 cups diced
  pineapple (fresh or
  canned)

1 cup plain
  unsweetened
  coconut milk

2 lime wedges

1 Add the basil leaves to the juicer, followed by the pineapple.

2 Pour into two glasses, stir half of the coconut milk into each glass, add a squeeze of fresh lime juice, and serve.

144 CALS PER SERVING   **3 MIN**   **4 INGREDIENTS**

Nutrition per serving
2g fat (2g saturated fat), 0mg cholesterol, 38mg sodium,
32g carbohydrate, 1g protein

APPLE CINNAMON TODDY

This sweet and spicy juice is combined with brewed tea and can be enjoyed warm or over ice. Cinnamon has been found to help stabilize blood sugar levels. However, it can add quite the kick to this drink, so use it sparingly.

Makes: about 2 servings

Serving size:
 12fl oz (355ml)

2 medium Granny Smith apples, stemmed, cored, and halved

2 cups hot brewed tea (green tea or herbal orange tea recommended)

1 tsp ground cinnamon

1 Add the apples to the juicer.

2 Pour into two glasses, add a cup of the brewed tea to each glass, and add half of the cinnamon to each glass. Stir and serve. (Alternatively, allow to cool and serve over ice.)

 121 CALS PER SERVING

 5 MIN   3 INGREDIENTS

Nutrition per serving
0g fat (0g saturated fat), 0mg cholesterol, 9mg sodium, 32g carbohydrate, 1g protein

STRAWBERRY ORANGE MINT

Cool and refreshing mint (an underappreciated herb) gets to shine in this pretty blush-colored juice. You'll experience floral notes and juicy bursts of flavor with every sip.

Makes: about 2 servings

Serving size:
 8fl oz (235ml)

3 cups fresh
  strawberries, hulled

1 medium navel
  orange, peeled

10 fresh mint leaves

1 Add the strawberries to the juicer, followed by the orange and mint leaves.

2 Pour into two glasses and serve.

 **117 CALS** PER SERVING

 5 MIN

3 INGREDIENTS

Nutrition per serving
1g fat (0g saturated fat), 0mg cholesterol, 6mg sodium,
28g carbohydrate, 3g protein

C.C.A.P.

This refreshing blend features celery, cayenne, apple, and pear, but I make it so often at our house that it's known simply by its acronym. You'll find this one being requested quite often!

Makes: about 2 servings

Serving size:
 10fl oz (295ml)

1lb (450g) celery hearts

2 medium pears, stemmed, cored, and halved (Bartlett variety recommended)

2 medium apples, stemmed, cored, and halved (Gala or Red Delicious varieties recommended)

1 medium lemon, peeled

2 pinches cayenne pepper

1 Add the celery hearts to the juicer, followed by the pears, apples, and lemon.

2 Pour into two glasses, stir in a pinch of cayenne pepper, and serve.

 **282 CALS** PER SERVING

 5 MIN

 **5 INGREDIENTS**

Nutrition per serving
1g fat (0g saturated fat), 0mg cholesterol, 127mg sodium,
72g carbohydrate, 3g protein

HONEY LIMEADE

Limes don't yield a large quantity of juice, but their flavor is unmistakable. Drizzle in some natural sweetness from honey and you'll have the freshest limeade ever!

Makes: about 2 servings

Serving size:
 12fl oz (355ml)

1 medium lime,
 peeled

1 tbsp honey

24fl oz (700ml)
 water

Lime slices, to serve

1 Add the lime to the juicer, then add the honey and stir well.

2 Add half of the water to each glass and stir until the honey is dissolved.

3 Garnish with lime slices and serve over ice.

 42 CALS PER SERVING   5 MIN   **3 INGREDIENTS**

Nutrition per serving
0g fat (0g saturated fat), 0mg cholesterol, 1mg sodium,
12g carbohydrate, 0g protein

CARDAMOM DREAMS

This blend may, in fact, be my favorite juice of all time. The unexpected combination of ingredients builds into a mountain of flavors that gets more special with each sip.

Makes: about 2 servings

Serving size:
 10fl oz (295ml)

½ medium unpeeled
 English cucumber

1 medium pear,
 stemmed, cored,
 and halved
 (Bartlett variety
 recommended)

3 cups diced fresh
 pineapple

½ tsp ground
 cardamom

1 Add the cucumber to the juicer, followed by the pear and pineapple.

2 Stir in the cardamom, pour into two glasses, and serve.

 **167 CALS** PER SERVING

5 MIN

 **4 INGREDIENTS**

Nutrition per serving
0.5g fat (0g saturated fat), 0mg cholesterol, 5mg sodium,
46g carbohydrate, 2g protein

PEAR BANANA SPIRULINA SHOOTER

This sweet and sassy shooter has a vibrant color and is perfect for a shot of energy before a workout, or for an afternoon pick-me-up. Use green or blue spirulina to boost the nutrient content.

Makes: about 2 servings

Serving size:
4fl oz (120ml)

2 large, very ripe pears, stemmed, cored, and halved (Bartlett variety recommended)

1 medium banana, peeled

1 medium lime, peeled

2-inch piece fresh ginger root, peeled

1 tsp spirulina powder

1 Add the pears to the juicer, followed by the banana, lime, and ginger root.

2 Stir in the spirulina powder, pour into two glasses, and serve.

 138 CALS PER SERVING

🔪 10 MIN

 5 INGREDIENTS

Nutrition per serving
0.5g fat (0g saturated fat), 0mg cholesterol, 16mg sodium, 32g carbohydrate, 2g protein

SWEET POTATO CINNAMON SHOT

This tastes like Thanksgiving in a glass! A light dusting of cinnamon completely changes the way this juice tastes. If you are a latte fan, try it with a few dashes of pumpkin spice blend.

Makes: about 2 servings

Serving size:
  2.5fl oz (75ml)

2 medium sweet
  potatoes, peeled
  and chopped
  (about 1lb/450g)

½ tsp ground
  cinnamon

1 Add the sweet potatoes to the juicer.

2 Pour into two glasses, sprinkle the cinnamon over the top, and serve.

 103 CALS PER SERVING

 3 MIN

 **2 INGREDIENTS**

Nutrition per serving
0g fat (0g saturated fat), 0mg cholesterol, 41mg sodium,
24g carbohydrate, 2g protein

JUICY WATERMELON WATER

Inspired by my favorite cold-pressed bottled juice, this blend is extra hydrating and beyond refreshing. The base recipe can be enhanced with ginger, cayenne, or lime, depending on your preferences.

Makes: about 2 servings

Serving size:
 12fl oz (355ml)

3 cups diced watermelon

1 apple, stemmed, cored, and halved (Gala or Red Delicious varieties recommended)

2 celery stalks

1 cup plain, unsweetened coconut water

1 Add the watermelon to the juicer, followed by the apple and celery stalks.

2 Stir in the coconut water, pour into two glasses with ice, and serve.

156 CALS PER SERVING

5 MIN

4 INGREDIENTS

Nutrition per serving
0.5g fat (0g saturated fat), 0mg cholesterol, 162mg sodium, 37g carbohydrate, 3g protein

PASSION CUCUMBER NECTAR

This frothy, golden juice blend has a tropical feel. Ginger adds a hint of spice and highlights the sweetness of the mango and passion fruit.

Makes: about 2 servings

Serving size:
  12fl oz (355ml)

1 medium passion fruit, halved, and pulp and seeds scooped out

1-inch piece fresh ginger root, peeled

2 cups diced fresh mango

2 medium unpeeled English cucumbers

1 Add the passion fruit pulp and seeds to the juicer, followed by the ginger root, mango, and cucumbers.

2 Pour into two glasses and serve.

 153 CALS PER SERVING

 5 MIN

 **4 INGREDIENTS**

Nutrition per serving
1g fat (0g saturated fat), 0mg cholesterol, 9mg sodium, 38g carbohydrate, 3g protein

BLOOD ORANGE BEET

Earthy beets have met their match—sweet blood orange! Beets and celery also contain natural compounds that help lower blood pressure.

Makes: about 2 servings

Serving size:
12fl oz (355ml)

2 large beets, peeled

2 medium blood oranges, peeled and halved

1 medium Granny Smith apple, stemmed, cored, and halved

1lb (450g) celery hearts

1 Add the beets to the juicer, followed by the blood oranges, apple, and celery hearts.

2 Pour into two glasses and serve.

200 CALS PER SERVING   **10 MIN**   **4 INGREDIENTS**

Nutrition per serving
1g fat (0g saturated fat), 0mg cholesterol, 129mg sodium, 48g carbohydrate, 5g protein

MANGO POP!

This mild blend of mango and cucumber gets a huge pop of flavor from juicy pineapple and spicy ginger. The ingredients in this juice also contain potent inflammation-fighting compounds.

Makes: about 2 servings

Serving size:
 10fl oz (295ml)

1 medium unpeeled
 English cucumber

2 cups diced fresh
 mango

1 cup diced fresh
 pineapple

1-inch piece fresh
 ginger root, peeled

1 Add the cucumber to the juicer, followed by the mango, pineapple, and ginger root.

2 Pour into two glasses and serve.

 168 CALS
PER SERVING

 10 MIN

 4 INGREDIENTS

Nutrition per serving
1g fat (0g saturated fat), 0mg cholesterol, 6mg sodium,
42g carbohydrate, 3g protein

ORANGE TURMERIC BLAST

Turmeric is the "it" spice for good reason: it's a powerful antioxidant and is known to combat inflammation. The earthy flavor of this golden spice combines nicely with the natural sweetness of the carrots, pineapple, and orange to create a powerfully delicious blend.

Makes: about 2 servings

Serving size:
 8fl oz (235ml)

1 medium navel
 orange, peeled

2 cups chopped
 fresh pineapple

4 medium carrots

2 tsp ground
 turmeric

Pinch black pepper
 (optional)

1 Add the orange to the juicer, followed by the pineapple and carrots.

2 Whisk in the turmeric and black pepper (if using), pour into two glasses, and serve.

 183 CALS PER SERVING

 5 MIN

 **5 INGREDIENTS**

Nutrition per serving
0.5g fat (0g saturated fat), 0mg cholesterol, 87mg sodium,
46g carbohydrate, 3g protein

ORANGE FLAX MANGO

OJ fans, this juice is for you! Juicy citrus freshness takes center stage, while flaxseeds help thicken this juice and add a nutty background flavor.

Makes: about 2 servings

Serving size:
 8fl oz (235ml)

2 medium navel
 oranges, peeled
 and halved

2 cups diced fresh
 mango

1lb (450g) celery
 hearts

4 tsp ground
 flaxseeds

1 Add the oranges to the juicer, followed by the mango and celery hearts.

2 Stir in the flaxseeds, pour into two glasses, and serve.

 **246 CALS** PER SERVING   🔪 **5 MIN**   **4 INGREDIENTS**

Nutrition per serving
2.5g fat (0.5g saturated fat), 0mg cholesterol, 84mg sodium,
54g carbohydrate, 5.5g protein

NECTARINE AND TOMATO "SALAD"

Inspired by my favorite salad, this unlikely combination is an explosion of fresh summer flavors. Essential oils in the mint infuse the juice with a sweet minty heat.

Makes: about 2 servings

Serving size:
10fl oz (295ml)

1 large beefsteak tomato, halved

5 fresh mint leaves

1 medium unpeeled English cucumber

2 medium nectarines, pitted and halved

1 Add the tomato to the juicer, followed by the mint, cucumber, and nectarines.

2 Pour into two glasses and serve.

106 CALS PER SERVING   **10 MIN**   **4 INGREDIENTS**

Nutrition per serving
1g fat (0g saturated fat), 0mg cholesterol, 11mg sodium, 25g carbohydrate, 4g protein

BERRY BELL PEPPER

This vibrant red juice contains nearly six times the recommended daily amount of vitamin C, which can help minimize the symptoms of a cold by reducing inflammation in the throat and nasal passages.

Makes: about 2 servings

Serving size:
 8fl oz (235ml)

1 cup fresh
 strawberries, hulled
 (roughly 8 medium
 strawberries)

3 red bell peppers,
 stemmed and
 seeded

1 medium Gala
 apple, stemmed,
 cored, and halved

1 Add the strawberries to the juicer, followed by the bell peppers and apple.

2 Pour into two glasses and serve.

 138 CALS
PER SERVING

5 MIN

 3 INGREDIENTS

Nutrition per serving
1g fat (1g saturated fat), 34mg cholesterol, 6mg sodium,
34g carbohydrate, 3g protein

SWEET CUCUMBER GINGER

A hint of sweetness from optional sugar or agave nectar will help bring out the flavors of both the cukes and the fresh ginger in this drink, which is best served chilled over crushed ice.

Makes: about 2 servings

Serving size:
  8fl oz (235ml)

2-inch piece fresh
  ginger root, peeled

2 medium unpeeled
  English cucumbers

2 tsp sugar or agave
  nectar (optional)

1 Add the ginger to the juicer, followed by the cucumbers.

2 Pour the juice into two glasses filled with crushed ice. Stir a teaspoon of the sugar or agave nectar (if using) into each glass, then serve.

38 CALS PER SERVING   **5 MIN**   **3 INGREDIENTS**

Nutrition per serving
0g fat (0g saturated fat), 0mg cholesterol, 3mg sodium,
10g carbohydrate, 1g protein

PART 5

GREEN JUICES

BEET GREENS WITH GREEN APPLES

Don't throw away those beet greens! Those feathery, green, red-veined leaves contain just as many vitamins and minerals as the beets themselves. The tangy edge of green apple helps balance the earthy flavor.

Makes: about 2 servings

Serving size:
 6fl oz (175ml)

2 medium green apples, stemmed, cored, and halved

1 bunch beet greens (with stems)

1 Add the apples to the juicer, followed by the beet greens.

2 Pour into two glasses and serve over ice or well chilled.

 57 CALS PER SERVING

5 MIN

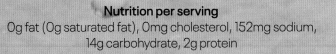 **2 INGREDIENTS**

Nutrition per serving
0g fat (0g saturated fat), 0mg cholesterol, 152mg sodium,
14g carbohydrate, 2g protein

GREEN LEMONADE

A slight deviation from your typical juice blend, the juicer is used to make a nutrient-rich base that is then diluted with water, sweetened with honey, and poured over ice. This green twist on lemonade is incredibly refreshing!

Makes: about 2 servings

Serving size:
 12fl oz (355ml)

1 bunch kale, rinsed
 and large stems
 removed

3 cups chopped
 romaine lettuce

1 large lemon,
 peeled

2 tbsp honey

2 cups cold water

1 Add the kale to the juicer, followed by the romaine and lemon.

2 Pour the mixture into a pitcher and then stir in the honey and water.

3 Pour into two glasses over ice and serve.

 109 CALS PER SERVING

 10 MIN

 **5 INGREDIENTS**

Nutrition per serving
1g fat (0g saturated fat), 0mg cholesterol, 100mg sodium,
25g carbohydrate, 5g protein

TOMATILLO APPLE FENNEL TONIC

This juice offers up an explosion of flavors and an electric green color from the tomatillos. Plus, the fennel and apple combo helps optimize digestion.

Makes: about 2 servings

Serving size:
 6fl oz (175ml)

3 medium
  tomatillos, husks
  removed

1 fennel bulb,
  trimmed and
  quartered

3 medium apples,
  stemmed, cored,
  and halved (Gala or
  McIntosh varieties
  recommended)

1 Add the tomatillos to the juicer, followed by the fennel and apples. (Adding the tomatillos to the juicer first will help prevent any sticky buildup in your juicer.)

2 Pour into two glasses and serve.

173 CALS PER SERVING

5 MIN

3 INGREDIENTS

Nutrition per serving
1g fat (1g saturated fat), 0mg cholesterol, 61mg sodium,
45g carbohydrate, 3g protein

KIWI LIME CHIA AGAVE

Adding chia seeds to fresh juice provides texture and supplies a boost of heart-healthy, brain-boosting omega-3 fats.

Makes: about 2 servings

Serving size:
 5fl oz (150ml)

6 kiwi fruit, peeled

1 medium lime,
 peeled

2 tsp chia seeds

2 tsp agave nectar

1 Add the kiwi fruit to the juicer, followed by the lime.

2 Stir in the chia seeds and agave nectar, wait 2-3 minutes for the seeds to gel, then pour into two glasses and serve.

 **199 CALS**
PER SERVING

5 MIN

 **4 INGREDIENTS**

Nutrition per serving
3.5g fat (0g saturated fat), 0mg cholesterol, 8mg sodium,
44g carbohydrate, 4g protein

KALE AND CANTALOUPE WITH LIME

This fruit and veggie combo is a match made in heaven! Don't be deterred by the color—this juice is addictive. A squeeze of lime on the finish makes it extra tasty and also delivers an additional shot of vitamin C.

Makes: about 2 servings

Serving size:
 8fl oz (235ml)

3 cups chopped
 cantaloupe

1 bunch kale, rinsed
 and stemmed

½ medium lime,
 peeled

2 lime wedges

1 Add the cantaloupe to the juicer, followed by the kale and lime.

2 Pour into two glasses, add a squeeze of lime to each glass, and serve.

 131 CALS PER SERVING

 5 MIN

 **3 INGREDIENTS**

Nutrition per serving
0.5g fat (0g saturated fat), 0mg cholesterol, 82mg sodium,
30g carbohydrate, 5g protein

WHEATGRASS CITRUS SHOT

Wheatgrass is high in vitamins K and E, and various B vitamins, and also contains a concentrated dose of chlorophyll, which promotes healthy blood. Look for fresh wheatgrass at health-food stores, or buy your own plants online and grow it indoors.

Makes: about 2 servings

Serving size:
 2fl oz (60ml)

1 cup roughly
 chopped
 wheatgrass
 (rinse wheatgrass
 thoroughly before
 chopping)

1 large navel orange,
 peeled

2 lime wedges

1 Add the wheatgrass to the juicer, followed by the orange.

2 Pour into two glasses, add a squeeze of lime to each glass, and serve.

 **40 CALS** PER SERVING

8 MIN

 **3 INGREDIENTS**

Nutrition per serving
0g fat (0g saturated fat), 0mg cholesterol, 8mg sodium,
8g carbohydrate, 2g protein

ROMAINE APPLE BREEZE

This ultra-refreshing green juice has just the right amount of sweetness and acidity. The high water content in romaine lettuce makes it ideal for juicing and it adds all kinds of fresh flavor to this recipe.

Makes: about 2 servings

Serving size:
 6fl oz (175ml)

4 cups chopped
 romaine lettuce

2 medium green
 apples, stemmed,
 cored, and halved

1 Add the lettuce to the juicer, followed by the apples.

2 Mix gently with a spoon, pour into two glasses, and serve.

 89 CALS
PER SERVING

 5 MIN

 2 INGREDIENTS

Nutrition per serving
0g fat (0g saturated fat), 0mg cholesterol, 4mg sodium,
24g carbohydrate, 2g protein

GREEN GRAPE SPRITZER

Warning! This will ruin all bottled grape juice—forever.
The grape juice contains a lot of natural sugars, so the seltzer
water is added to impart a little fizz, and also to help cut the
intense sweetness of the grapes.

Makes: about 2 servings
Serving size:
 10fl oz (295ml)

3 cups green grapes
1 cup plain seltzer

1 Add the grapes to the juicer, then stir in the
seltzer.

2 Pour into two glasses and serve.

 92 CALS
PER SERVING

2 MIN

 **2 INGREDIENTS**

Nutrition per serving
0.5g fat (0g saturated fat), 0mg cholesterol, 3mg sodium,
24g carbohydrate, 1g protein

HONEYDEW BANANA SPINACH COCKTAIL

This green drink is the ideal pairing of leafy greens and juicy sweetness. Bananas don't yield a lot of volume, but their essence is powerful; to maximize the flavor, run the banana through the juicer first, followed by the other ingredients.

Makes: about 2 servings

Serving size:
 10fl oz (295ml)

1 medium banana, peeled

½ honeydew melon, chopped (about 3 cups)

4 cups baby spinach

1 Add the banana to the juicer, followed by the melon and spinach.

2 Pour into two glasses and serve.

158 CALS PER SERVING

8 MIN

3 INGREDIENTS

Nutrition per serving
1g fat (0g saturated fat), 0mg cholesterol, 94mg sodium,
39g carbohydrate, 4g protein

PARSLEY PINEAPPLE SHOT

You won't be able to get enough of this bright and uplifting punch of pineapple and parsley. Use the leaves and stems of the parsley, as they both are juicer-friendly and filled with nutrients.

Makes: about 2 servings

Serving size:
 4fl oz (120ml)

2 cups fresh parsley
 (leaves and stems)

2 cups diced fresh
 pineapple

1 Add the parsley to the juicer, followed by the pineapple.

2 Pour into two shot glasses and serve.

104 CALS
PER SERVING

5 MIN

2 INGREDIENTS

Nutrition per serving
0g fat (0g saturated fat), 0mg cholesterol, 36mg sodium,
25g carbohydrate, 3g protein

GREEN CARROT

Carrots go green for this emerald-colored treat! For even brighter flavor, add a few handfuls of fresh parsley.

Makes: about 2 servings

Serving size:
 10fl oz (295ml)

1lb (450g) carrots

4oz (115g)
 watercress

2 cups baby spinach

2 medium apples,
 stemmed, cored,
 and halved (Gala or
 Red Delicious
 varieties
 recommended)

1 Add the carrots to the juicer, followed by the watercress, spinach, and apples.

2 Pour into two glasses and serve.

233 CALS PER SERVING   **5 MIN**   **4 INGREDIENTS**

Nutrition per serving
1g fat (0g saturated fat), 0mg cholesterol, 128mg sodium,
55g carbohydrate, 6g protein

SPINACH TANGERINE

This is a refreshing fruit juice hiding in a green cloak! This might look like a traditional green juice, but each refreshing sip features a burst of bright and tangy citrus.

Makes: about 2 servings

Serving size:
4fl oz (120ml)

2 large tangerines, peeled

4 cups baby spinach

1 Add the tangerines to the juicer, followed by the baby spinach.

2 Pour into two glasses and serve.

 102 CALS PER SERVING

 5 MIN

 **2 INGREDIENTS**

Nutrition per serving
0g fat (0g saturated fat), 0mg cholesterol, 221mg sodium, 26g carbohydrate, 4g protein

SPINACH CUCUMBER

Cucumbers are high in water content, so they're perfect for juicing. Leave the skins intact to elevate the antioxidant content. The aroma of cucumber can also promote relaxation.

Makes: about 2 servings

Serving size:
 12fl oz (355ml)

2 medium unpeeled
 English cucumbers

2 cups baby spinach

1 Add the cucumbers to the juicer, followed by the spinach.

2 Pour into two glasses and serve.

 52 CALS PER SERVING   **5 MIN**    **2 INGREDIENTS**

Nutrition per serving
0.5g fat (0g saturated fat), 0mg cholesterol, 30mg sodium,
12g carbohydrate, 3g protein

SWISS APPLE PUNCH

The best thing about an underappreciated leafy green like Swiss chard is the leaves and stems are both edible. Less bitter than kale, chard mingles nicely with apple and a hint of lemon.

Makes: about 2 servings

Serving size:
 8fl oz (235ml)

1 bunch Swiss chard
 (leaves and stems)

2 apples, stemmed,
 cored, and halved
 (Gala or Red
 Delicious varieties
 recommended)

1 medium lemon,
 peeled

2 tsp honey

½ cup cold water

1 Add the Swiss chard to the juicer, followed by the apples and lemon.

2 Stir in the honey and water, then pour into two glasses and serve.

 **160 CALS** PER SERVING   **5 MIN**    **5 INGREDIENTS**

Nutrition per serving
0.5g fat (0g saturated fat), 0mg cholesterol, 98mg sodium,
41g carbohydrate, 2g protein

APRICOT CANTALOUPE WITH KALE

Tangy apricot and smooth melon help mellow out the bitter edge of kale in this well-balanced beverage. This recipe also works well with honeydew melon or yellow watermelon.

Makes: about 2 servings

Serving size:
 8fl oz (235ml)

2 medium apricots,
 pitted

3 cups diced fresh
 cantaloupe

2 cups chopped
 fresh kale

1 Add the apricots to the juicer, followed by the cantaloupe and kale.

2 Pour into two glasses and serve.

 **129 CALS** PER SERVING

 5 MIN

 **3 INGREDIENTS**

Nutrition per serving
0.5g fat (0g saturated fat), 0mg cholesterol, 67mg sodium,
30g carbohydrate, 4g protein

ELECTRIC SPINACH

Yellow grapefruits are more acidic and tangier than pink or red varieties, but they make a delectable green juice when paired with spinach and apple. The high doses of vitamin C in this recipe help make the iron in the spinach more absorbable.

Makes: about 2 servings

Serving size:
  8fl oz (235ml)

1 medium yellow
  grapefruit, peeled
  and halved

3 cups baby spinach

3 medium red
  apples (Gala variety
  recommended),
  stemmed, cored,
  and halved

1 Add the grapefruit to the juicer, followed by the spinach and apples.

2 Pour into two glasses and serve.

206 CALS PER SERVING   **5 MIN**   **3 INGREDIENTS**

Nutrition per serving
1g fat (0g saturated fat), 0mg cholesterol, 39mg sodium,
53g carbohydrate, 3g protein

CELERY SPINACH SIPPER

Is a green juice spinach or celery? How about a blend of both?! Mild, smooth, and verdant, this low-calorie juice supplies 10 percent of your daily iron needs.

Makes: about 2 servings

Serving size:
 8fl oz (235ml)

3 cups baby spinach

1lb (450g) celery hearts

1 Add the spinach to the juicer, followed by the celery hearts.

2 Pour into two glasses and serve.

 47 CALS
PER SERVING

 5 MIN

 **2 INGREDIENTS**

Nutrition per serving
0.5g fat (0g saturated fat), 0mg cholesterol, 183mg sodium,
8g carbohydrate, 3g protein

KALE APPLE CARROT

This juice is green, mean, and loaded with beta-carotene! This blend is energizing, refreshing, and has just the right balance of fruit and veggie flavors.

Makes: about 2 servings

Serving size:
 10fl oz (295ml)

1lb (450g) carrots

1 bunch kale
 (12oz/340g), rinsed
 and stems removed

1 clementine, peeled

2 medium apples,
 stemmed, cored,
 and halved (Gala or
 Red Delicious
 varieties
 recommended)

1 Add the carrots to the juicer, followed by the kale, clementine, and apples.

2 Pour into two glasses and serve.

 292 CALS
PER SERVING

5 MIN

 4 INGREDIENTS

Nutrition per serving
0.5g fat (0g saturated fat), 0mg cholesterol, 117mg sodium,
70g carbohydrate, 7g protein

KIWI APPLE ROMAINE

This green blend combines kiwi and romaine to create a vitamin A-rich powerhouse. Keep the kiwi skins intact to take full advantage of all the nutrients they contain.

Makes: about 2 servings

Serving size:
 8fl oz (235ml)

2 medium Granny
 Smith apples,
 stemmed, cored,
 and halved

3 large unpeeled
 kiwi fruit, halved

4 tightly packed
 cups chopped
 romaine lettuce

1 Add the apples to the juicer, followed by the kiwi fruit and romaine lettuce.

2 Pour into two glasses and serve.

 162 CALS
PER SERVING

 5 MIN

 3 INGREDIENTS

Nutrition per serving
1g fat (0g saturated fat), 0mg cholesterol, 9mg sodium,
41g carbohydrate, 2g protein

WATERMELON CUCUMBER WATERCRESS SIPPER

Uber-refreshing and immensely hydrating, this electrolyte-filled drink has just a hint of sweetness. Thanks to the watercress, this blend also contains nearly twice your daily recommended dose of vitamin K to help keep your bones and blood healthy.

Makes: about 2 servings

Serving size:
  12fl oz (355ml)

3 cups fresh
  watercress (about
  4oz/115g)

5 fresh mint leaves

4 cups cubed fresh
  watermelon

1 medium seedless
  cucumber

1 Add the watercress to the juicer, followed by the mint leaves, watermelon, and cucumber.

2 Pour into two glasses and serve.

 136 CALS
PER SERVING

 10 MIN

 **4 INGREDIENTS**

Nutrition per serving
0.5g fat (0g saturated fat), 0mg cholesterol, 58mg sodium,
38g carbohydrate, 5g protein

INDEX